IMAGES OF ENGLAND

SOLDIERS OF SHROPSHIRE

Soldiers of Bridgnorth Company, Shropshire Rifle Volunteers, in camp at Ludlow in 1886.

IMAGES OF ENGLAND

SOLDIERS OF SHROPSHIRE

PETER DUCKERS FOR THE
SHROPSHIRE REGIMENTAL MUSEUM

Guns of the Shropshire Royal Horse Artillery training near Ellesmere in July 1941.

First published in 2000 by Tempus Publishing

Reprinted in 2010 by
The History Press
The Mill, Brimscombe Port,
Stroud, Gloucestershire, GL5 2QG
www.thehistorypress.co.uk

British Library Cataloguing in Publication Data.
A catalogue record for this book is available from the British Library.

ISBN 978 0 7524 1866 7

Typesetting and origination by
Tempus Publishing.
Printed and bound in Great Britain by
Marston Book Services Limited, Didcot

Contents

Shropshire Yeomanry – the Guard of Honour at the wedding of Capt. D.U. Corbett in 1959.

Introduction

Intended as a companion to the Tempus publication of photographs of the King's Shropshire Light Infantry (the county's Regular regiment from 1881-1968), the present compilation offers a glimpse into the history of the volunteers of Shropshire. These were the 'part-time soldiers' of the Militia, the Rifle Volunteers, the Territorials, the Yeomanry and the Artillery who served their county and their country in peace and war. In addition to these, wartime demands led to the creation of a range of other military and associated formations – such as the Home Guard, Civil Defence groups, nursing, ambulance and fire-fighting units, the Women's Land Army, the Auxiliary Territorial Service and many other training, administrative and support organizations.

From Anglo-Saxon times, English counties maintained some form of Militia. This force consisted of men who were required to undertake regular military training in case they were needed in time of invasion or war. Later, lists of eligible men were kept in each parish and the men selected (by ballot) had to undergo a number of days of training every year (usually over three years) and attend annual camps. A chosen man could avoid Militia service only if he found a replacement. The Militia was at its height during the Napoleonic Wars, when many more men were 'called up'; their role was to serve in garrison areas, to free Regulars for overseas service and to provide drafts into the Regulars as required. Thus, units of the Shropshire Militia found themselves in Southern Ireland (1812-14). They were also called up or 'embodied' during the Crimean War and the Boer War. In 1852, the compulsory element of Militia service was abolished and all recruits were volunteers. A man might join the Militia if he wanted rather more military training or accepted the possibility of seeing 'active service' overseas, since the Militia remained an important source of replacements and reinforcements for Regular Battalions. With the extensive army reforms of 1907/08, the Militia was redesignated as the Special Reserve and the Shropshire Militia became the 3rd (Special Reserve) Battalion of the KSLI. During the Great War it served as a training and draft-finding unit based in Ireland and effectively ceased to exist in 1919.

While there had always been a volunteer element in the Militia, the Volunteer movement as such – men who came forward freely to offer themselves for military training – really dates from the French Wars of 1793 to 1815. The prospect of French invasion led to the formation of hundreds of volunteer units throughout the country – infantry, cavalry and artillery – whose job it would largely be to defend their own area against attack. They can therefore be regarded as a form of 'Home Guard', as distinct from the Militia who could be called upon to serve beyond their county (though not on campaign service). In Shropshire's towns and rural districts, many distinctive units were raised, with typically exotic titles – the Loyal Morfa Legion, the Oswestry Rangers, the Brimstree Loyal Legion, the Loyal Newport Volunteers (see p. 128) and many more. At the close of the French Wars, these Volunteer units were all disbanded, with the exception of some of the cavalry elements which came to form the Shropshire Yeomanry.

The renewed fear of French invasion in 1859 led to the rapid re-establishment of Volunteer units throughout the country. In Shropshire, eighteen Volunteer Rifle Companies were formed, with each major town raising its own company of eighty to a hundred men. These Rifle Volunteer companies were eventually grouped to form the 1st and 2nd Volunteer Battalions of the KSLI and in 1908, with the formation of the Territorial Force, became the 4th (Territorial) Battalion, King's Shropshire Light Infantry. As such, they served with distinction through both World Wars and continued to exist until 1967 when they were disbanded. Their eventual successors as Territorial Infantry in Shropshire were the 5th (Shropshire and Herefordshire) Light Infantry (Volunteers), themselves disbanded in 1999. The old Rifle Volunteer tradition is now perpetuated in 'E' (Rifle) Company, The Mercian Regiment, TA, based at Copthorne Barracks, Shrewsbury.

The mounted element of the Napoleonic volunteer movment, the Yeomanry Cavalry, survived army reductions after 1815. The Shrophsire Yeomanry can trace its origins to the formation of the Wellington Troop in 1795. By 1814, the various Yeomanry units had been reduced to three distinct corps: the North Shropshire, the Shrewsbury and the South Shropshire Yeomanry Cavalry. These were reduced by amalgamation in 1828 to form the North Salopian Yeomanry Cavalry and the South Salopian Yeomanry Cavalry and these in turn amalgamated to become the Shropshire Yeomanry Cavalry in 1872. Designated as Imperial Yeomanry in 1900, its volunteers served as the 13th (Shropshire) Company, 5th Battalion, Imperial Yeomanry, during the South African War and went on to campaign in Egypt, Palestine and France in the First World War. Converted to Artillery in 1940, the Shropshire Yeomanry served during the Second World War in North Africa and Italy. As a result of TA reductions, they became part of the Mercian Yeomanry in 1971 and now exist as part of the Royal Mercian and Lancastrian Yeomanry.

There had been Volunteer Artillery units in Shropshire during the Napoleonic Wars, but they were all disbanded by 1815. In 1860, during the Volunteer revival, one Rifle Volunteer Company (the 9th Shrewsbury) converted to artillery as the Shropshire Artillery Volunteers. This was later designated 1st (Shropshire and Staffordshire) Artillery Volunteers but in 1908 severed its connection with Staffordshire to become the Shropshire Royal Horse Artillery. Its function was to provide an artillery arm to the newly-formed Welsh Border Mounted Brigade of Yeomanry. The Shropshire RHA fought on the Western Front (1914-18) and in North Africa, Italy and North-West Europe during the Second World War. The unit retained its separate existence until 1967, when it was absorbed into the Shropshire Yeomanry.

The various volunteer units really were 'Soldiers of Shropshire' – they were local men who gave up their time to train and exercise and learn the art of war in case they should ever be needed. When the requirements of war demanded their service, they fought alongside their Regular comrades in South Africa, in the Great War and through the Second World War. Today, though much reduced, the old volunteer spirit is perpetuated within the county in the form of the Shropshire Yeomanry element of the Royal Mercian and Lancastrian Yeomanry, and a Rifle Company of The Mercian Regiment, TA. At least a part of their proud heritage is reflected in the photographs presented in this book.

Peter Duckers
Shrewsbury, November 1999

Acknowledgements

The compilier would like to thank the Trustees of the Shropshire Regimental Museum for permission to publish the photographs held in the Regimental Museum in Shrewsbury Castle. In addition, he would like to thank the following individuals for their help with text and details: Maj. J.York MBE, BA, Maj. P. Graham TD, the late Capt. J. Webb, Mr P. Downward, Mr J. Backhouse, Mr F. Bayliss, Mr L. Stocking, Mr S. Martin, Mr W. Jones, Mr J. Taylor and other members of the Staff of the Regimental Museum.

One

Soldiers
of Shropshire

An officer of the Shropshire Yeomanry in review order, c. 1900.

Officers of the Shropshire Militia, c. 1856. The Militia served to provide reinforcements and to free Regular units for overseas service in time of war. After 1852, the Militia was made up of volunteers. Its officers were usually local gentlemen of property appointed by the Lord Lieutenant, with Regular Army officers and NCOs attached for administrative and training purposes. Their uniform was basically the same as that worn by Regulars and here shows a mixture of the double-breasted tunic of 1855 and the single-breasted version of 1856. Also visible is the tall shako (leather helmet) of 1855-61.

A private soldier of the Shropshire Militia, c. 1855, showing the arrangement of belts, packs and pouches. The Shropshire Militia was embodied during the years 1854-56 while the Crimean War was being fought. (From a watercolour by William Sharpe.)

Officers of the North Salopian Yeomanry Cavalry, *c*. 1870. The North and South Salopian Yeomanry were formed in 1828 as amalgamations of existing county Yeomanry units. The officers shown here wear single-breasted dark blue tunics with silver braid and buttons and white cross-belts. Some have the unusual black leather helmet worn by the NSYC in the period 1864-72. In 1872 the North and South Salopian Yeomanry amalgamated to form the Shropshire Yeomanry Cavalry.

SHROPSHIRE
VOLUNTEER RIFLE CORPS.

Hundred of Shrewsbury

ALL Parties willing to become Members of the Volun
Rifle Corps within the Hundred of Shrewsbury, or other
to concur in promoting this patriotic measure, are respect
and earnestly invited forthwith to intimate the same to
either personally or in writing, so that their names may
transmitted to the Lord Lieutenant, previously to the hol
of a Public Meeting to consider the regulations for
formation and management of the Force.

Further information may be obtained at my Office.
By Order,

J. J. PEELE,

Sub-division Cl

Guildhall,
30th May, 1859.

RICHARD DAVIES, PRINTER, 7 HIGH STREET SHREWSBURY

In 1859, with the fear of war with France, there was a nationwide revival of the Volunteer movement, which had fallen into abeyance after 1815. The Rifle Volunteers were a form of 'home guard' who would not be called upon to serve beyond their own area. Eighteen companies were raised in Shropshire in 1859-60, with every major town having its own Company – Shrewsbury, Bridgnorth, Whitchurch, Oswestry, Wem, Ellesmere etc.

The Shropshire Rifle Volunteer companies were grouped to form the 1st and 2nd Volunteer Battalions of the King's Shropshire Light Infantry in 1888. Shown in camp at Towyn in 1890 are soldiers of Bridgnorth Company, 1st Volunteer Battalion. The soldier on the far left wears a fine array of shooting awards.

Soldiers and Bandsmen of a company of the 2nd Volunteer Battalion in their distinctive drab grey uniform with black facings. They wear the low 1869 pattern shako and carry Snider-Enfield rifles.

In 1860, the 9th (Shrewsbury) Company, Rifle Volunteers, converted to Artillery as the 1st Shropshire Volunteer Artillery Corps. Officers and men in a variety of uniforms, including white fatigues, pose around their guns on the artillery training fields at Monkmoor, c. 1870. Note the borough policemen in top hats.

Officers and a Bugler of the Shropshire Artillery Volunteers outside the new drill-hall in King Streeet, Wellington, c. 1880. The SAV had elements in Shrewsbury, Wellington and Church Stretton. Surgeon H.J. Rope, second left, wears a cocked hat; most of the others wear the new 1878 home-service helmet.

The 1st Shropshire Artillery Volunteers on exercise, c. 1890. Brigaded with the Worcestershire, the Cheshire and the Staffordshire Artillery Volunteers in their early days, the Shropshire AV were formally brigaded with the Staffordshire Artillery Volunteers in 1880. Each unit comprised four batteries of guns and approximately 320 men. The Shropshire Artillery HQ was in Coleham, Shrewsbury. Shown here are gun teams drawing Armstrong field guns and ammunition limbers.

The Shropshire Yeomanry parading in dress uniform in The Square, Shrewsbury, c. 1895. In the centre, with the breast badge of the Order of St Patrick, is the commanding officer, Lt-Col. the Earl of Kilmorey. Commissioned into the Yeomanry in 1865, he became Commanding Officer in 1889. The circumstances of this parade are not recorded, though it may be associated with the celebrations of the 100th anniversary of the founding of the Shropshire Yeomanry, the first troops having being raised in Market Drayton and Wellington in 1795.

Pte R. Gough in the very practical khaki service dress worn between 1900 and 1902 by the Shropshire Yeomanry volunteers who served in the South African War. Designated as Imperial Yeomanry from 1900 (to allow service overseas), Shropshire Yeomen served as the 13th (Shropshire) Company of the 5th Battalion, IY.

An example of the Certificate of Service given to members of the Shropshire Imperial Yeomanry as a permanent record of their time with the regiment. This one was awarded to Pte Walter Cobb for service between 1906 and 1908.

CERTIFICATE
OF
SERVICE

This is to Certify

that *Private Walter Cobb.*

served in *Shropshire Imperial Yeomanry* from the *Seventeenth* day of *March* 1906 till the *Thirty-first* day of *March* 1908 having served continuously for *Two* years *Fifteen* days.

Corps in which service was given
Shropshire Imperial Yeomanry.

Campaigns and Medals
nil

Charles Burnett LT-GENERAL.
COMMANDING-IN-CHIEF WESTERN COMMAND

'Why should Whitchurch tremble?' The 3rd (Whitchurch) Company, Shropshire Rifle Volunteers, outside the Egerton Hall, *c.* 1900. They wear the grey and black uniform adopted by the eight Shropshire rifle companies which had been brought together in 1888 to form the 2nd Volunteer Battalion, KSLI.

RSM Charles Sheppard (left) in the uniform of the 12th (Wem) Company, Shropshire Rifle Volunteers, *c.* 1888. This is a fine study of the uniform of the companies comprising the 2nd Volunteer Battalion. The uniform is officially described as gray or drab, with braid, facings and leather equipment in black.

Shropshire Rifle Volunteers in the later pattern service dress with slouch-hat, of the Boer War era, *c.* 1904. The various Shropshire Rifle Volunteer units supplied men to form two Volunteer Service Companies, each serving for one year in South Africa, attached to the 2nd Battalion, the King's Shropshire Light Infantry. These men served with the 1st Volunteer Service Company (1900/01) and wear the ribbon of the Queen's South Africa Medal.

The 3rd (Special Reserve) Battalion, King's Shropshire Light Infantry, on parade in The Square, Shrewsbury, during the visit of King George V in 1914. The old county Militia was reformed as the Special Reserve as part of the Haldane reforms of 1907/08 which established the Territorial Force.

The Sergeants' Mess of the 3rd (Special Reserve) Battalion, 1917. The Battalion saw no active service during the First World War. Stationed in South Wales and Ireland, it served in a training and draft-supplying role with nearly 17,000 officers and men passing through its ranks during the course of the war.

Ross Troop of the Shropshire Yeomanry ready for war in 1914. Photographed in training at Flixton in 1914, they wear the standard post-1902 khaki service dress with puttees, leather bandoliers and peaked caps.

New recruits into the 4th (Territorial) Battalion, the King's Shropshire Light Infantry, in 1914. The army reforms of 1908 converted the old Rifle Volunteers into the Territorial Force and the two Shropshire Volunteer Battalions were combined to become the 4th KSLI.

Drivers of the Shropshire Royal Horse Artillery, c. 1914. The 1908 army reforms separated the Shropshire Artillery Volunteers from their Staffordshire colleagues. They were re-designated as Horse Artillery, to enable them to act in support of the newly-formed Welsh Border Mounted Brigade.

Men of the Shropshire Royal Horse Artillery in 1917. Despite their title, they actually served as Field Artillery, on the Western Front, as 'A' Battery, 293rd Brigade, Royal Field Artillery. A second war-raised unit served as 'A' Battery, 158th Brigade.

'Shrewsbury Knuts': the 2nd/4th Battalion, KSLI, was a second-line unit established to train men for the 4th KSLI and other battalions. It saw no active service, being based on the Isle of Man and on the east coast of England before disbandment in December 1917.

Although less well known than its Second World War counterpart, the Women's Land Army was formed during the First World War to free men for war service. Miss Elsie Gray (of Shrewsbury) wears the working outfit, badges and armband of the WLA; she worked at 'the Leas', Queen's Head, Oswestry from 1917 to 1919 (see also p. 31).

Volunteers and Reserves: during the First World War a complicated array of local volunteer units was formed. Shown in The Quarry, Shrewsbury, are men of the National Reserve (formed in 1909 from the Veteran Reserve). They were a patriotic body of former officers and soldiers too old for active service but used in home-guard, training, draft-conducting and recruiting roles. Another such unit was the Shropshire Volunteer Training Corps which also served as a form of home guard.

COUNTY OF SALOP VOLUNTEERS.

To *J. Morgan* of *Shrewsbury*

I, GEORGE CHARLES HERBERT, EARL OF POWIS, Lord Lieutenant of the County of Salop, acting as President of the Grand Council of the County of Salop Volunteer Regiment, and acting on the advice of Captain Beville Stanier, M.P., Regimental Commandant of the Shropshire Volunteer Regiment, do hereby approve the appointment of you, the said *J. Morgan* to be *Platoon Commander* in the *Shropshire* Volunteer Corps under the command of *Col. H. J. Hope-Edwards* acting as *Commandant Southern Battalion* thereof.

AND you, the said *J. Morgan* are to observe and follow such orders and directions from time to time as you shall receive from your Regimental Commandant or any other your Superior Officer, according to the rules and customs of War in pursuance of the trust hereby reposed to you.

SIGNED BY ME *Powis.* at *Walcot* in the County of *Salop* this *30th* day of *September* in the year of our Lord one thousand nine hundred and *fifteen*

A rare survival: a Lord Lieutenant's commission for the Shropshire Volunteers. In 1916, the Shropshire Volunteer Training Corps became the 1st (Northern) and 2nd (Southern) Battalion, Shropshire Volunteer Regiment. This commission, signed by the Earl of Powis, appoints Mr J. Morgan to the Southern Battalion.

National Reservists in Wem: a 'broomstick parade', 1914-15, so-called because the men had no weapons other than broom-handles (and no uniforms, as is apparent in the photograph). Made up of men who were too old or unfit for military service, the National Reserve served as a 'home guard'.

Shropshire Volunteer Training Corps: uniformed and civilian staff of the SVTC in Shrewsbury in 1918. A mixture of men in uniform and out, women and boy-scouts who served on the administrative staff of the 1st Battalion, Shropshire Volunteers.

Larking about for the camera: men of the Shropshire Yeomanry in a post-war camp in Attingham Park. On the piano is Tpr D. Rawbone, with Sgt G. Martin sitting on the bench, Sgt Edgar Hopley on the extreme right and Tpr Arnold Embrey (top centre) with cap raised.

The machine-gun platoon of 4th KSLI (under Lt Quinn, mounted) in camp at Tenby in 1933. After the First World War, the Territorial Battalion returned to its usual round of training and annual camps.

Ludlow Platoon, 4th KSLI, on army maneouvres in Hampshire, 1935. They still wear the old khaki service dress uniform, but with collar badges restored in the 1920s. Notice the bicycles to the left which were used for relaying messages.

At war again: 4th KSLI under Lt-Col. H.H. Lanyon being inspected by HRH the Duke of Gloucester, accompanied by Brigadier J.G. Bruxner Randall. The men wear the newly-introduced battle-dress uniform with blouse, gaiters and webbing equipment designed in 1937 and introduced from 1937 to 1940.

Criftin's Company, 2nd (Oswestry) Battalion, Shropshire Home Guard, 1943. On formation in May 1940 the Shropshire Home Guard (raised from the Local Defence Volunteers) was affiliated to the Shropshire Territorial Army Association and was badged as King's Shropshire Light Infantry.

Some of Meole Brace Home Guard outside the Brooklands Hotel. Left to right, back row: J. Milne, F. Potter, P. Walton, W. Hammond. Front row: G. Potter, Jack and Len Ramshore. By December 1944, when the force was stood down, 31,000 men had served in the Shropshire Home Guard.

'E' (Coton Hill) Company, 1st Battalion Shropshire Home Guard, marching up Castle Street, Shrewsbury, for the Armistice Day parade in 1943. In the front is Maj. Key and behind him CSM Stone. Leading to left and right are Lt Cole and Lt Rogers.

Air Raid Precautions: although Shrewsbury was never seriously threatened by air attack, the threat of air bombardment and gas attack early in the war had to be taken seriously. Local ARP services were formed and trained; here they practise respirator drill.

Civil Defence: many factories and businesses set up their own fire-fighting and rescue teams to deal with the possible results of aerial bombing. These men are the Rescue team ('R' on helmets) for Messrs Chatwood at Harlescott, Shrewsbury. The team leader wears a white helmet.

A Civil Defence Corps rescue team practises the evacuation of casualties from a bomb-damaged building. In the event, air-raid damage to Shrewsbury was minimal, with only two incidents recorded, when German aircraft 'dumped' their bomb loads near the railway station and north of the town.

The Women's Land Army: Miss Barbara Price (daughter of Elsie Gray on p. 23) in Land Army uniform. The WLA was larger and more effectively organized during the Second World War than in 1917/18. Miss Price worked at 'Home Farm', Little Wenlock and at Moreton Hall, Llynclys, Oswestry.

The Shropshire Royal Horse Artillery training at Stone in Staffordshire in October 1939. The battery was by this time designated 240th (Shrops. RHA) Battery in the 51st Medium Regiment, Royal Artillery. After training, it went to France with the British Expeditionary Force in February 1940.

The Yeomanry as gunners. Converted to Artillery in January 1940, the Shropshire Yeomanry formed 101st and 102nd Batteries, 75 Medium Regiment, and 112th and 113th Batteries, 76 Medium Regiment, RA. This group shows men of the Yeomanry in 75th Medium Regiment during training at Builth Wells in August 1941.

The side to beat: the football team of the 20th Infantry Training Centre, Shrewsbury, 1944/5. The 20th ITC was set up at Ditherington and Copthorne Barracks to train men for the King's Shropshire Light Infantry and North Staffords. The ITC base at the Flax Mill in Ditherington, famous as the world's first iron-framed building, still stands. The team featured here included top-rate players: Billy Wright of Wolves and England (middle row, third from right); Johnny Hancock of Wolves and England (middle row, third from left); Roy Brown of Stoke (back row, fourth from right), Percy Lovett of Everton (back row, fifth from left) and W. Richardson of West Bromwich and England (front row, centre).

Colour Party of the 4th KSLI at St Chad's Church, Shrewsbury, during the dedication of the Regimental Chapel in 1951. This was the first occasion in which the Colours were carried after the war. The Regimental Colour (right) carries the rosette of French Croix de Guerre ribbon commemorating the Battalion's gallantry at Bligny in 1918 (see p. 115).

Shropshire Yeomanry in camp in Norfolk in 1952. They wear the 1949 pattern battle-dress with the black beret introduced in the late 1940s. After a post-war reduction in numbers, the Shropshire Yeomanry was up to 300 officers and men by 1952.

Maj. P. Graham (far left) with men of Shropshire Royal Horse Artillery, at Larkhill camp, 1966. From 'suspended animation' in 1945, they became 'P' Heavy Battery, 639 Heavy Regiment, RA (Territorial Army) when the TA was re-formed in 1947.

The Cambrian March, 1963: the Shropshire Yeomanry team poses for the local press before starting on the 24-hour competitive 'slog' centred around Cader Idris. It was an annual event for units of the 53rd Welsh Division. Far left is RSM Stan Mitchell, Queen's Dagoon Guards.

Officers mainly of the Shropshire Yeomanry, the Queen's Dragoon Guards and the Pembroke Yeomanry. The association with the QDG began in 1959, when their Head Quarters was established in Shrewsbury, and from 1961 to 1967, the Pembroke Yeomanry was affiliated to the Shropshire Yeomanry.

Some of The Light Infantry Volunteers, effectively the successor to the 4th KSLI, which was disbanded in 1967. Men of HQ (Shrewsbury) and 'C' Coy (Hereford), seen here under the command of Lt Darby and Lt Rafield were the winners of the 'Best Volunteer Unit' cup in 1967.

The 5th Battalion, Light Infantry (Volunteers). The old Volunteer tradition in the county passed into the hands of the 5th Light Infantry in 1973. This Territorial Army unit was itself disbanded in 1999.

A familiar sight at many local functions was the Bligny Band and Bugles of the 5th Light Infantry, based at Copthorne Barracks, Shrewsbury. Their title recalls the battle in 1918 for which the old 4th KSLI was awarded the French Croix-de-Guerre (see p. 115). Bugle Major Robinson is in the foreground.

The 95th (Shropshire Yeomanry) Signal Squadron, Royal Signals, formed out of the Shropshire Yeomanry as a result of army reorganization in 1969. They parade along Shrewsbury High Street on 30 April 1995 during the ceremonies for the granting of the Freedom of Shrewsbury to the Shropshire Yeomanry. The unit was disbanded in 2009.

The Shropshire Yeomanry became part of the Mercian Yeomanry in 1971, which was itself absorbed into the present Royal Mercian and Lancastrian Yeomanry. The Shropshire Yeomanry troops of the RMLY parade along High Street, Shrewsbury, on 30 April 1995, having been granted Freedom of Entry on their 200th anniversary.

Two

Uniforms

An invitation to the Shropshire Yeomanry ball in 1886, showing a Sergeant in other-ranks' full dress (left) and a Corporal in stable dress.

Sir George Harnage of Bridgnorth Troop, South Salopian Yeomanry Cavalry, c. 1870. The South Salopian Yeomanry was formed in 1828 and wore red tunics with gold braid and buttons, where the North Salopian wore dark blue with silver fittings.

Lt-Col. the Earl of Kilmorey in the officers' dress uniform of the Shropshire Yeomanry Cavalry. The SYC was formed in 1872 by the amalgamation of the North and South Salopian Yeomanry. The new uniform combined elements of both earlier forms, with blue tunic and gold braid. The helmet is the silver Albert pattern with red and white horsehair plume.

R.D. Scott Evans of Baschurch in the other-ranks' full-dress uniform of the Shropshire Yeomanry, c. 1885. The other-ranks' uniform lacks the elaborate gold braiding seen on the officers' version (see previous page). The elderly gentleman, perhaps Evans' father, wears medals for the Crimean War.

J.W. Downes, Shropshire Yeomanry, in review dress as Royal Escort at Bangor, in 1911, when King George V presented a new Guidon (Colour) to the regiment. Downes had a distinguished career, taking him through the ranks of the Rifle Volunteers, the Shropshire Yeomanry in South Africa and Egypt and eventually to the command of an infantry battalion (1917-19) earning the DSO and MC.

Officers and NCOs of the 1st Volunteer Battalion, KSLI, in camp at Tasley, Bridgnorth, c. 1884. Most of the NCOs on the back row wear the scarlet serge tunic of Regular Army pattern, with the spiked blue-cloth helmet introduced in 1878. The officers on the front row (including Capt. R.H. Colley in the centre) wear dark-blue patrol jackets and forage caps. Volunteer units tended to wear white or silver badges, buttons and fittings to distinguish them from Regulars who usually wore gold, gilt or brass. The medical officer sits at the front, far right.

Medical orderlies and stretcher-bearers of 1st Volunteer Battalion, KSLI, *c.* 1890. The other ranks in scarlet serge wear the distinctive helmet-plate of the Army Medical Corps and red-cross arm badges. The officers wear blue patrols, one with forage cap and one with side-cap, bearing the KSLI (Volunteers) badge.

A daguerrotype portrait of George Evans, watchmaker and jeweller of Oswestry, of the 15th (Oswestry) Rifle Volunteers prior to 1880. He wears the distinctive uniform and glengarry cap adopted by the rifle companies of the 2nd Volunteer Battalion. This was an early form of camouflage and was adopted by many volunteer rifle units throughout the country.

Cpl Henry Hall of the Ludlow Company, 2nd Volunteer Battalion. In this photograph from 1905 (a late appearance of this uniform) he is shown as winner of the Shropshire Rifle Association Challenge Cup; the other shooting awards on his tunic and sleeve testify to his prowess as a marksman. The cup is now on display in the Regimental Museum in Shrewsbury Castle.

Capt. F.C. Mein, 15th (Oswestry) Company, Adjutant of the 2nd Volunteer Battalion. This is a fine study of the officer's uniform of the rifle companies comprising the Battalion. Their uniform (subdued grey and black) reflected their associations as 'Rifle' regiments. The Meins were a distinguished military family, many of whom served in the Indian Army.

J.A. Allison, a young Bugler of the 1st Volunteer Battalion, photographed in 1903. He wears the typical full dress scarlet serge uniform of the Battalion, with the distinctive striped shoulder wings worn by musicians.

Lt-Col. William Field, first commanding officer of the Shropshire Artillery Volunteers, c. 1872. He wears the full dress of the Royal Artillery, with busby, and carries a magnificent sword presented by the SAV in 1864. This is now in the Regimental Museum in Shrewsbury Castle (see p. 122).

Staff Sgt Ecclestone, Shropshire Artillery Volunteers, as Artillery Volunteers' Champion Shot, with trophies. He wears typical Royal Artillery collar badges and helmet plate, with the 'ball' finial to the helmet, which for Corps (like the Royal Artillery) replaced the 'spike' on the home-service helmet in 1881 (see earlier version on p. 14). He wears the Volunteer Long Service and Good Conduct medal, introduced in 1894.

Medical orderlies and stretcher-bearers of the 1st Shropshire and Staffordshire Artillery Volunteers, c. 1890. They wear standard Volunteer Artillery uniforms and helmet-plates (compare with those of 1st Rifle Volunteers, p. 43).

Bandsmen and soldiers of Wem Company, 2nd Volunteer Battalion, KSLI, under Maj. W. Baxter (front row, centre) in Wem Grammar School yard, 1903. A muster of seventy-nine out of the ninety-three officers and men of the company. A few wear the ribbon of the Queen's South Africa medal having served in the Volunteer Service Company during the Boer War.

Private M.T. Davies, 1st Volunteer Battalion and 4th KSLI, c. 1910. Note the marksman's badge (crossed rifles), the chevron indicating two years' service in the TA and the three stars, each representing five years in the Volunteer force. (Seventeen years' service is thus indicated.)

Sgt H.T. Manning, Shropshire Royal Horse Artillery, at the outbreak of war in 1914. By this time, the Volunteers wore the standard Royal Artillery uniform of the Regulars but with the silver or white-metal badges and lace which distinguished Volunteer units (see also p. 55).

Pte J.R. Jones in the service dress with bandolier and slouch-hat worn during the Boer War, when volunteers of the Shropshire Yeomanry served as 13th Company of the 5th Battalion, Imperial Yeomanry.

Maj. R.A. Newill (right), commanding the Shropshire Royal Horse Artillery, 1908. Newill, a solicitor from Wellington, served for over thirty years with the Shropshire Artillery. He wears the full dress of the Royal Horse Artillery (introduced in 1908) and has the Volunteer Officers' Decoration among his medals.

Maj. R.A. Newill in standard officers' khaki service dress, c. 1914. Newill served long enough to lead the Shropshire Royal Horse Artillery to war in August 1914 but was forced by ill health to relinquish command of the battery in the early days of the conflict.

Tropical kit: a soldier of the Shropshire Yeomanry in Egypt, September 1916. Serving as dismounted troops in Egypt and Palestine (1916-18), they amalgamated with the Cheshire Yeomanry to form the 10th Battalion, KSLI, and served on the Western Front in 1918.

Walter Thomas Rogers, Shropshire Yeomanry. The 'Imperial Service' badge over his right pocket indicates that he has volunteered to serve overseas. Rogers later served with 2/1st Shropshire Yeomanry (a training unit) in Ireland and was drowned returning home in October 1918 when the mail-steamer *Leinster* was torpedoed in the Irish Sea.

Before: Pte. G.W. Cooke, Shropshire Yeomanry, ready for war in 1914. A detailed view of the arms and equipment carried by a Yeoman and his horse when ready for 'active service'.

After: G.W. Cooke in Egypt as a trooper in the Imperial Camel Corps, 1916. A few men of the Shropshire Yeomanry served in the ICC as part of the 2nd (British) Battalion serving in the Sinai desert. This was a far cry from the fields and lanes of Shropshire!

Pte George H. Chester, 4th KSLI, in typical coarse khaki service dress of the First World War. He wears the soft cap with ear-flaps, nicknamed the 'gor-blimey', possibly after the comments of the first Sergeant Major to see them!

The Band of the 4th KSLI in front of the Shwe Dagon Pagoda, Rangoon, 1914. The Territorial Battalion had an exotic start to the war – service in the Far East (Andaman Islands, Rangoon, Hong Kong, Singapore) and South Africa before encountering 'real' warfare on the Western Front in October 1917.

NCOs of the Shropshire Yeomanry as Guard of Honour at the wedding of Sir Baldwin Leighton Bt in 1932. Sir Baldwin commanded the Shropshire Yeomanry from 1933 to 1937. Most wear medals for the First World War, many with the Long Service and Good Conduct medal. They carry the 1908-pattern cavalry sword.

Soldiers of the Shropshire Yeomanry in August 1941, by which time they had been dismounted and converted to artillery in 75th and 76th Medium Regiments, Royal Artillery. Most of these men of the 75th wear the new battle-dress with gaiters and side-caps introduced around 1939.

Revd J.M. Haddow of Falkirk, Battalion Chaplain, preaching to men of the 4th KSLI in Holland, 1944. They wear battle-dress with the unpopular 'cap, general service', later replaced by the beret. Note the green backing to the cap badge and the shoulder-flash of the 11th Armoured Brigade.

Shropshire Royal Horse Artillerymen marching along High Street, Shrewsbury on an Armisitice day parade, c. 1960. They wear the 1949-pattern battle-dress uniform and beret with smaller Royal Artillery badge. Some wear medals for the Second World War and the Terriorial Efficiency Medal.

In camp with the 4th KSLI, 1959: Bugler Stokoe (left) and Bandmaster W. Dennett MBE, MSM, ARCM. Dennett had a distinguished army career of nearly fifty years, serving in the 4th Dragoon Guards, the 2nd KSLI and the 4th KSLI. He died in 1991 aged ninety-three.

Former Battery Sgt-Maj. H.T. Manning, who served in the Shropshire RHA during the First World War, presents his dress tunic to the regimental collection in 1964 (see p. 48). He is seen here with Maj. P. Graham, Shropshire RHA. In the foreground is the 1868 Hill-Trevor Cup of the Shropshire Artillery Volunteers.

Uniforms of the 4th KSLI, 1961. Left to right: CQMS Ron Gough in battle dress; the other-ranks full-dress uniform of 1908-14; RQMS Bob Williams in No. 1 Dress; CSM George Morgan in No. 2 Dress.

Historic uniforms and other artefacts of the Shropshire Rifle Volunteers and 4th KSLI on display during a recruiting drive in Bridgnorth in 1961.

Major P. Graham (front row, fifth from left) with officers and men of the Shropshire Royal Horse Artillery at Larkhill Camp in 1966. This was the penultimate camp of the Shropshire RHA. In 1967, they were absorbed into the Shropshire Yeomanry and effectively ceased to exist as a separate unit, 107 years after formation. WO Ball is fourth from the left on the front row.

A variety of uniforms including mess-dress, worn by officers of The Light Infantry Volunteers in camp in 1971. Front row, fourth from left, is General Sir Geoffrey Musson, Colonel of the KSLI from 1963 to 1968 and Colonel, The Light Infantry, from 1968 to 1972.

Soldiers of The Light Infantry Volunteers 'clearing weapons' in camp at Gaerloch Head in 1970. They wear Combat Dress and carry the Self Loading Rifle (SLR) introduced from 1955. Replaced by the SA80 rifle from 1980 onwards, the SLR is still widely used by other armed forces.

Mounted and dismounted troopers of the Shropshire Yeomanry at the re-opening of Shrewsbury Castle in 1995. This is a rare sighting of the full-dress uniform, which has not changed in over a hundred years. In the background are American re-enactors of 'HM's 53rd Regiment of Foot in America'.

Three

Arms
and Equipment

A 5 inch howitzer of the Shropshire Royal Horse Artillery being towed through Shrewsbury, c. 1934.

Muzzle-loading 64-pounder 'position guns' of the Shropshire Artillery Volunteers on specially-built platforms on Long Mynd, near Church Stretton, *c.* 1875. When originally established, the Shropshire Artillery Volunteers were designated as Garrison Artillery i.e. using heavy guns meant for static defence or siege warfare. As can be seen from the photograph, their training exercises were social occasions! The site of the emplacements remains identifiable and fragments of shells fired during practice are still found on the hilltops nearby.

An early photograph of the band of the Shropshire Artillery Volunteers – with some very young musicians! – under Bandmaster Bowdler at Murivance, Town Walls, Shrewsbury, *c.* 1880.

Men of the Shropshire and Staffordshire Artillery Volunteers on exercise, c. 1890. The field-gun is an Armstrong rifled breech-loader. The corporal (left) wears his rank badge on his pill-box cap as well as on his sleeve – a style used by Artillery units at that time.

They do work ... firing the Armstrong guns. These 15-pounder guns, introduced in 1885, replaced muzzle-loaders which had remained in use well into the 1880s. They were kept in service, especially with the Volunteers, until the early years of this century.

Shropshire Imperial Yeomanry in camp at Oswestry, 1905. This is the gun section, showing the .303 Maxim gun, on tripod stand, introduced as the standard machine-gun of the British army in 1890. It remained in service until gradually replaced by the Vickers after 1912.

The gun section of 3rd (Special Reserve) Battalion, KSLI, 1910. They are armed with the Maxim machine-gun, here shown on its wheeled and armoured mobile carriage. Most British battalions were equipped with two machine-guns by 1914.

The 15-pounder Erhardt quick-firing field gun. Introduced in 1901 is was largely replaced by the 18-pounder for Regular Field Artillery units after 1906 but was used by the Shropshire RHA (and other Territorial artillery units) with great effect throughout the First World War.

A field gun used in a recruiting or fund-raising campaign in Castle Square, Ludlow during the First World War. As a point of interest, the soldier behind the gun wears the distinctive cap-badge of the Birmingham Battalions of the Royal Warwickshire Regiment.

A soldier of the Shropshire Yeomanry: W.K. Butler at Cloverley Camp, Whitchurch, May 1904. By this time, the Shropshire Yeomanry carried the standard infantry rifle, the 'long' Lee Enfield, not a smaller cavalry carbine version. This photograph clearly shows the 'shoe' which secured the rifle butt when not in use.

The motorcycle section of the Shropshire Yeomanry, probably at Flixton in 1915. These men, who owned their own motorbikes, were used as messengers and dispatch riders. The motorcycles are mainly Douglas's and a Rudge and four have consecutive licence numbers.

A 5 inch howitzer of the Shropshire RHA near the drill-hall in Coleham, Shrewsbury, which they shared with 4th KSLI. By this time (around 1934) they bore the unwieldy designation 240th (Shropshire RHA Battery, 60th (6th Cheshire and Shropshire) Medium Regiment, Royal Artillery (Territorial Army).

An experiment to try to tow a howitzer of Shropshire RHA up to the Long Mynd by tractor and lorry in the 1930s – with a great deal of help from 'interested bystanders'.

Part of the Signal Section of the Shropshire Yeomanry during the annual camp held at Attingham Park in 1935. They display various methods of conveying messages and signals: motor cycles, semaphore flags, heliographs and morse keys.

Farewell to the horse: Market Drayton, 1940. When the Shropshire Yeomanry was designated as an artillery unit, it ceased to have a military use for its horses. In March 1940, they were handed over to the Cheshire Yeomanry, which briefly retained its mounted role.

Guns and trucks of the 240th (Shropshire Royal Horse Artillery) Battery, then part of 51st (Midland) Medium Regiment, Royal Artillery, training for war at Colemere, near Ellesmere, in July 1941. The battery arrived in Egypt in October 1942.

Training at Colemere: 5.5 inch howitzers of 240th (Shropshire Royal Horse Artillery) Battery in 1941. The battery went on to serve with distinction in Italy in from 1943 to 1945 and was based in Germany by the end of the war.

A party of local school-girls inspecting a Royal Artillery anti-aircraft gun during a display of Air Raid Precautions just before the outbreak of war.

A searchlight on caterpillar tracks being examined by local dignitaries as part of Shropshire's anti-aircraft defences early in the war.

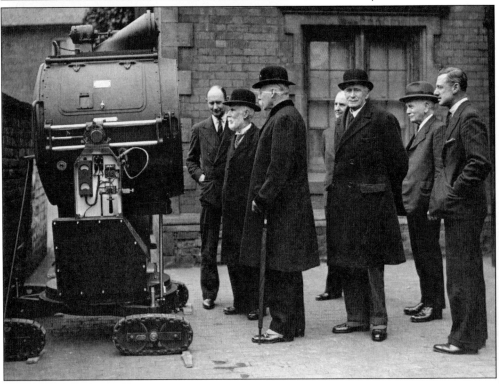

The Band of the Shropshire Yeomanry, c. 1950. The band – a familiar sight at camps, regimental functions and local social gatherings – was originally a heavy drain on the Officers' Mess funds, but later was at least partly funded by the local County Territorial Association.

Capt. Wace with National Servicemen under training with the Shropshire Royal Horse Artillery late in 1953. National Service continued after the war (two years' service) until it was phased out in 1960.

Schoolboys pose on a 155mm self-propelled gun of the Shropshire Royal Horse Artillery in 1958. 639 Heavy Regiment RA (with the Shropshire RHA as 'P' Battery) was the only Territorial unit to use this gun – which was a novel sight on the roads around Shrewsbury.

The Annual Camp of the Shropshire Royal Horse Artillery at Westdown in 1958. This 'end of camp' photograph shows the 155mm self-propelled guns of 'P' (Shropshire RHA) Battery with 'R' Battery, 639 Heavy Regiment.

Territorials of the 4th KSLI during field training in the 1959 camp, learning to use the 3.5 inch rocket-launcher. CSM Jones is seen as the loader.

Officers and men of the Shropshire Yeomanry (foreground) in November 1963 pictured with one of their Ferret scout cars and Series II Land Rovers.

Light Infantry Volunteers training at Gaerloch Head in 1970. The soldier on the left fires the Self Loading Rifle. On the right is the General Purpose Machine Gun (GPMG) introduced in 1962.

Sgt Keith Willocks, 5th Light Infantry, the Champion Shot at the West Midlands District Meeting, Lichfield, 1973. He wears the 1968 pattern combat-dress in camouflage 'DPM' – 'disruptive pattern material' – and is armed with the SLR.

Four

On Active Service

Leaving for South Africa: a sketch showing the first contingent of Shropshire Imperial Yeomanry entraining at Shrewsbury station, 1900.

The Yeomanry return home in 1902. Attended by their colleagues in full dress (with band) men of 13th (Shropshire) Company, 5th Battalion Imperial Yeomanry, assemble outside Shrewsbury station. Three contingents of Shropshire Yeomanry were raised for service in South Africa, though only the first two actually served during the war, between 1900 and 1902. In a mounted infantry role, they served in the Cape Colony and in pursuit of fast-moving and elusive Boer commandos across the Orange Free State and the Transvaal during the arduous 'guerrilla war' phase of the campaign.

The summons to war: the 'call up' letter to L/Cpl Alan Butcher, Shropshire Yeomanry, requiring him to attend at the Drill Hall, Ludlow, on 5 August 1914 – the day after war was declared. They were ready to move only three days later.

No. 30   Army Form E. 635.

Territorial Force.

EMBODIMENT.

NOTICE TO JOIN.

No., Rank } *1393 Lance Cpl. A. Butcher*
and Name }

_____ Regt. or Corps.

Whereas the Army Council, in pursuance of His Majesty's

Proclamation, have directed that the **SHROPSHIRE YEOMANRY**

be embodied on the *5*

day of *August 1914*

You are hereby required to attend at *the Drill Hall Ludlow*

not later than _____ o'clock that day. Should you not present

yourself as ordered you will be liable to be proceeded against.

W.L. Kirby Adjutant.

Date *4. 8. 14*

An evocative snapshot showing 'C' Squadron, Shropshire Yeomanry, leaving Ludlow 'for active service' on 8 August 1914. Their mobilization was swift and efficient: this is only four days after the outbreak of war. After training at Oswestry, they initially headed for East Anglia and coastal defence duties.

Like generations of tourists before and after, these men of the Shropshire Yeomanry pose on camels in front of the Sphinx and the Pyramids of Giza. The Shropshire Yeomanry arrived in Egypt in March 1916 and although some of its men of did actually serve on camels (in the Imperial Camel Corps: see p. 51), the rest saw service in a dismounted role as infantry in the Senussi campaign in the Western Desert of Egypt and then against the Turks in Palestine. Amalgamated with the Cheshire Yeomanry to form the 10th KSLI, they left for France in May 1918.

A long way from Shrewsbury: a water-tank in the Western Desert. During the Senussi campaign in Egypt's Western Desert in 1916, men of the Shropshire Yeomanry fill up with water near the Temple of Jupiter Amon in the historic Suwa Oasis.

Men of 'C' (Ludlow) Squadron, Shropshire Yeomanry, probably at the Kharga Oasis in Palestine, December 1916. The men-by then serving as infantry- wear tropical kit with solar topees (pith helmets) against a very barren desert backdrop.

Recruits being inspected by HRH the Prince of Wales in Shrewsbury, *c.* 1915. As a depot town, Shrewsbury was a recruiting centre for a range of regiments and corps apart from those with county links. However, many of the men in this photograph were recruits for the Shropshire RHA.

War training: gunners of Shropshire Royal Horse Artillery practice with a field gun and ammunition limber. As 'A' Battery, 293 Brigade, Royal Field Artillery, it saw extensive service in France and Flanders, as did a war-raised second Shropshire RHA battery, which served as 'A'/158.

One of many: a memorial card for Maj. G.W. Jones, commanding 1st Shropshire Royal Horse Artillery. He was awarded the Military Cross for gallantry but was mortally wounded near Ypres in October 1917. He died on 10 November and was buried at Mendinghem, near Poperinghe.

In ever loving Memory of

George Worthington Jones,

Major Commanding
1st Shropshire Royal Horse Artillery,
Aged 31 years,
who died on the 10th November 1917,
from wounds received on
Sunday morning the 28th October,
when on Active Service with
The British Expeditionary Force.

Only Son of
Mr & Mrs R.E. Jones,
Oakley Grange,
Shrewsbury.

With
very sincere thanks
for kind sympathy.

Roll on Demob (i.e. demobilization and the return home): a group of Shropshire Royal Horse Artillerymen of 'A' Battery, 293rd Brigade, Royal Field Artillery, photographed in France towards the end of the war.

The 4th (Territorial) Battalion, KSLI, in Singapore in 1915. The 4th KSLI was sent overseas in October 1914, but its postings took it to various Far Eastern locations on garrison duty rather than on 'active' service. At Singapore, the 4th dealt with the mutiny of an Indian regiment in 1915 and escorted to Australia prisoners from the German warship *Emden*, sunk by the Australian ship *Sydney* off the Cocos Islands. After further training in South Africa, the 4th arrived in France in the autumn of 1917 to be pitched straight into the 3rd Battle of Ypres and the mud of Passchendaele.

Training in South Africa. The 4th arrived in Cape Town in May 1917, *en route* to England. However, with over 200 men ill with fever, the return home was delayed and the rest of the Battalion spent time digging trenches and training for trench warfare.

An open fire-trench with a bomb-proof dugout to the far right. Men of 4th KSLI under training in South Africa for Western Front conditions – but still in their tropical kit with shorts and sun-helmets.

Ellesmere Platoon, 4th KSLI in the khaki service-dress worn in France. The 4th Battalion arrived in England after three years abroad in July 1917, expecting home leave, but was sent straight to Le Havre and then to the Arras sector for training. It moved into the Ypres Salient in October.

Machine-gunners of the 4th Battalion in France, 1917. The Battalion could not have had a more demanding 'baptism of fire' on the Western Front, being pitched into the terrible fighting for Passchendaele. On its first day in action, 30 October 1917, the 4th Battalion lost 30 killed and 114 wounded.

A 1918 Christmas card of the 4th KSLI. It depicts the regimental cap-badge and the French Croix-de-Guerre avec Palme awarded to the Battalion as a unit for its gallantry in the taking of Bligny Hill on 6 June 1918 (see p. 115).

The 9th (Reserve) Battalion, KSLI, at Prees Heath Camp, Whitchurch, c. 1915. Prees Heath became a major training centre for a large number of regiments. The 9th KSLI, formed in November 1914, was another of the local war-raised battalions which trained recruits and posted them to their regiments. It did not serve overseas.

Pte. Alfred Evans, far right, with other recruits for the 6th KSLI at Blackdown Camp in 1914. The recruits wear emergency-issue blue serge uniforms distributed in November 1914 and are armed with obsolete rifles; recruits poured in so quickly that the demand for uniforms and equipment far exceeded supply.

Recruits for the 6th KSLI training at Blackdown Camp in 1914/5. 'C' (Shrewsbury) Company was a 'Pals' unit – local men who enlisted with their friends could serve together, a fact which interested the King when he inspected the 6th during training. The Battalion served entirely on the Western Front from July 1915.

No. 6 Platoon, 'B' Company, 6th KSLI in France, July 1917. They had just fought in the battle for Mount Sorrel (Ypres Salient) and then moved southwards to Serre in the Somme sector, where they took part in the attack on Guillemont.

A patriotic songbook published for, and dedicated to, the 'Pals' Company of the 6th KSLI. Such things were typical of the ephemera generated by the patriotic fervour of 'the Great War'.

A young-looking recruit into the 5th Battalion, KSLI. Raised on 6 August 1914 from 1st KSLI (i.e. the Regulars), the 5th was the first of Shropshire's 'war service' battalions. Thousands of local men flocked to join the 5th, which served entirely on the Western Front from May 1915.

Sgt G.E. Pope (from Much Wenlock) of the 1st and 5th KSLI. He wears the Distinguished Conduct Medal earned at Montbrehain in 1918 when, with two men, he attacked an enemy position, killing ten and capturing eighty, along with eight machine guns and a mortar He also wears the Military Medal and the 1914 Star.

'C' Company, 7th KSLI, marching out of Bournemouth *en route* to Aldershot in April 1915. Formed in Shrewsbury in September 1914, the 7th trained around Codford, Bournemouth and Aldershot before embarking for Boulogne in September 1915. They spent the entire war on the Western Front and suffered more casualties than any other KSLI battalion.

'My Pal': Pte. R.H.B. Smith of Malinslee, 7th KSLI. A veteran of the Boer War, Smith worked at Hadley Castle Works and re-enlisted in 1914. Awarded the Military Medal for gallantry at Arras, he was killed at Polygon Wood in September 1917, leaving a widow and seven children.

In France again: 240th (Shropshire RHA) Battery mixing with the locals in France in February1940. Leaving England with the British Expeditionary Force on 1 February, they were on the Maginot Line by April, where they received their 'baptism of fire'. Returning to the UK in June, they served until December on the east coast before returning to Ellesmere.

51st Medium Regiment, Royal Artillery (which included the Shropshire RHA) at Enfidaville, Tunisia, in 1943. The battery served in North Africa in support of the 8th Army from January to October 1943. It left for Italy in October 1943, landing at Salerno.

The HQ of 75th (Shropshire Yeomanry) Medium Regiment at Giza, with the obligatory photograph by the Pyramids (see p. 76). Leaving Liverpool in December 1942 for Durban, they reached Egypt in April 1943. After training, they moved through the desert to Tripoli before leaving for Sicily (and their first action) in August.

'C' Sub-section, 102nd Battery, 75th (Shropshire Yeomanry) Medium Regiment RA. The Shropshire Yeomanry formed 101st and 102nd Batteries in this Regiment. The group was photographed in Cairo in 1943, shortly before leaving for Italy.

The Shropshire Yeomanry in action. Both the 101st and 102nd Batteries saw their first fighting during the invasion of Sicily. Having landed near Syracuse, they were in action on the north-east of the island, where this photograph was taken in August 1943.

'The last barrage at Cassino'. The 75th and 76th Medium Regiments, RA, supported the 5th Army during the fighting for Monte Cassino in 1944, 'cracking the hardest nut in the Italian campaign'. The position was finally taken on 17 May, with the Shropshire Yeomanry providing part of the supporting artillery fire.

A 4.5" gun of the Shropshire Yeomanry in action against the Gothic Line. Deep mud was a constant problem. Infantry attacks were often held up by mud and weather, but the guns were kept in action, even when they had to be manhandled up steep slopes.

A gun of 76th Medium Regiment being re-assembled after repairs 'in the field', Italy, 1944. As the campaign progressed, there was a tendency for repairs to be carried out on the spot rather than the guns being sent behind the lines. All hands help swing the barrel into position after welding work had been completed.

Charges to pay

s.

RECEIVED

POST OFFICE TELEGRAM

Prefix. Time handed in. Office of Origin and Service Instructions. Words.

No. ___ 49

OFFICE STAMP

-1 SEP 39 SHREWSBURY SHROPSHIRE

From ___ 7.16 SHREWSBURY 16

To ___

Barnwell 87.

COMMANDING 4TH BN KSLI SHREWSBURY

MOBILIZE DATED 1/9/39 STOP INFORM DUPLICATE UNITS

STOP ACKNOWLEDGE

GENERAL SHREWSBURY.

Acknowledged 8·10pm.

Send (D) 4/KS61

8·7pm

B or C

For free repetition of doubtful words telephone " TELEGRAMS ENQUIRY " or call, with this form at office of delivery. Other enquiries should be accompanied by this form and, if possible, the envelope.

The terse telegram ordering the mobilization of the 4th (Territorial) Battalion, KSLI, on 1 September 1939, as the crisis with Germany deepened. The 'Duplicate Unit' referred to was another Territorial Battalion, the 2nd/4th KSLI, raised in March 1939 and re-named the 5th KSLI in September.

The 4th KSLI landed in Normandy on 14 June 1944 and took part in the fighting around Caen. Shown here are men mainly of the Anti-Tank Platoon in relaxed mood east of Le Beny-Bocage on 2 August. Pte Cramp 'entertains' his colleagues, which included Sgt Langford and Capt. L. Quash (front left).

The 4th KSLI with 3rd Royal Tank Regiment near La Ferroniere crossroads, during the advance southwards from Le Beny Bocage early in August 1944. The Battalion encountered some very tough pockets of resistance in this area and in the advance through Le Grand Bonfait and Aubusson.

'B' Company, 4th KSLI, on the march. The group includes CSM Baker, Sgt Murray, L/Cpl Geeson and Pte Norman. The Battalion fought its way into Belgium via Amiens 'with frequent small skirmishes'. From Antwerp, it wintered on the Maas and crossed the Rhine on 28 March 1945. It was the first British battalion to reach the Elbe.

The Liberation of Antwerp: carrier-borne troops of the 4th KSLI (the Mortar Platoon in this shot) as 'first into Antwerp' received a rapturous reception from the city population on 4 September 1944. But they faced heavy fighting in the city.

Happy, smiling faces: soldiers of 'C' Company, 4th KSLI line up for their rations near Duerne during the campaign in Holland in the winter of 1944.

Lt- Col. Max Robinson: second-in-command of the 4th KSLI when it landed in Normandy. He took over as Commanding Officer in September 1944, leading the 4th for the remainder of the campaign. He was awarded the DSO and bar, the Belgian Order of Leopold and the Croix-de-Guerre.

A Guard of Honour of the 4th KSLI under Maj. K. Chapman, awaiting inspection by the Prime Minister, Sir Winston Churchill, in November 1945 when he was presented with the Freedom of Antwerp. On the right is Capt. W.P. Cox MC, who later commanded the Battalion.

Some award winners of the 4th KSLI at Flensburg in June 1945. Left to right, back row: Pte Merrick (mentioned in dispatches), Sgt Hall (British Empire Medal), L/Cpl A. Satchel (Military Medal), Sgt Davies (Military Medal). Front row: Capt. Henry (mentioned in dispatches), Capt. Mearns (Medical Officer – mentioned in dispatches), Capt. J.M. Haddow (Chaplain – Military Cross), Lt-Col. M. Robinson (Distinguished Service Order and Bar), Sgt G. Eardley (Victoria Cross and Military Medal), CSM Baldwin (Military Medal), Lt Patch (mentioned in dispatches).

Five

Camps and Training

A comment on the rigours of training on Salisbury Plain!

1st Volunteer Battalion camp at Ludford Park, Ludlow, 1886. Volunteers could be called out only for local service but had to meet exacting standards before they were judged 'efficient'. They had to attend an annual camp (usually on a local landowner's estate) and undertake a certain number of days training each year.

Shropshire Imperial Yeomanry in camp at Brogyntyn Park, Oswestry, in 1905. This postcard shows the camp's portable smithy in action. Keeping the horses and their equipment up to standard required constant attention.

Shropshire Yeomanry on exercise: in their blue patrol uniforms, they mount a roadblock in Pontesbury. This was probably during the annual camp near Pontesford Hill in 1907. The Shropshire Yeomanry, affiliated to the Corps of Dragoons, trained as mounted infantry. This naturally did not exclude training in the use of the sword but did emphasize marskmanship and mobility. Training involved 'field days' (manoeuvres and exercises), competitions and sporting events (in which skills in swordsmanship and riding were developed), lectures, drills, parades and training in various skills such as musketry and signalling.

The Shropshire Royal Horse Artillery arrive for their annual camp at Parkgate in 1908. This was immediately after their designation as Royal Horse Artillery – so that they could provide an artillery arm to the new Welsh Border Mounted Brigade, a Yeomanry formation.

Sergeants of the Shropshire RHA on Salisbury Plain, 1912. Generally, the Volunteers and Yeomanry tended to do their annual training within Shropshire. The more specialist requirements of artillery training led the Shropshire RHA further afield, to ranges used by the Regular artillery for gunnery training and practice.

'Rough Riders' of the Shropshire Royal Horse Artillery during an annual camp before the war. These men were used as scouts and dispatch riders.

Shropshire Yeomanry at Walcot Park, 1912. The estate of the Earl of Powis, then Lord Lieutenant of Shropshire, Walcot Park was frequently used by the Yeomanry for camps and training. After 1908, the Shropshire Yeomanry formed part of the Welsh Border Mounted Brigade, which included the Shropshire RHA.

The Shropshire Royal Horse artillery 'under canvas' in camp at Hamilton in 1913 – actually their last peacetime camp. The men are shown here cleaning tack and saddlery.

A domestic scene in the annual camp of the Shropshire Yeomanry at Brecon in 1911. This year saw the presentation by King George V of a new Guidon (regimental Colour) to the Shropshire Yeomanry at Bangor; it was carried until 1959 (see pp. 113 and 121) and is now displayed in the Regimental Museum.

The endless round of cleaning: Shropshire Yeomanry in camp at Newton, Brecon, in 1911. They trained here with the Cheshire and Denbighshire Yeomanry, their colleagues in the Welsh Border Mounted Brigade. Exercises involved action against the South Wales Mounted Brigade.

'Spud bashing': the first post-war camp of the Shropshire RHA, Westdown, 1919. The end of the war saw a re-organization of the Territorial Force and the creation of the Territorial Army. In 1921, the Shropshire RHA was redesignated as Garrison Artillery and joined 60th Medium Brigade, RA (TA) as 240 (Howitzer) Battery.

Officers of the Shropshire Yeomanry in camp at Attingham Park, 1930. Training was carried out in the park and on Haughmond Hill. The annual sports were held in front of the house and included tent-pegging, mounted 'musical chairs', jumping in fours, and relay racing on horseback, motorcycle and foot.

The mounted trooper of the Shropshire Yeomanry between the wars. In khaki service dress with puttees, he looked very similar to his counterpart of pre-war days (see top p. 51). He carried the 1908-pattern cavalry sword and his rifle is housed in a holster.

Windmill Camp, Ludgershall, 1928. Training took place with the 6th Midland Cavalry Brigade: the Warwickshire, Staffordshire, Shropshire and Leicestershire Yeomanries, the Derbyshire Yeomanry Armoured Car Company and the South Notts Hussars (as artillery) – the only time the Shropshire Yeomanry trained with their brigade.

Divine Service in camp at Attingham Park conducted by the Yeomanry Chaplain, the Revd R.A. Giles, 1930. As usual, members of the public attended the service. Afterwards, the Meritorious Service Medal was presented to Squadron Sgt-Maj. Bosher and the Territorial Efficiency Medals to Sgt Austin and Trooper J. Brown.

Lowther Park, Penrith, 1939: the last mounted camp of the Shropshire Yeomanry. The approach of war led the Government to double the size of the Territorial Army. After heavy recruiting, the Shropshire Yeomanry was brought up to war establishment, with over 500 men and horses attending this camp.

The 4th KSLI cooks in 1935. As with the Territorial Artillery and Yeomanry, peacetime brought a return to the routine of annual camps and training. Far left : QM 'Sam' Caloe MBE, MSM, Belgian Croix-de-Guerre. He served for twenty-four years with the Territorial Army, having joined the 4th in 1917 from a Regular battalion.

Shropshire Yeomanry at Rolston, Hornsea, their first independent postwar camp, in 1950. Following war service as artillery, the Shropshire Yeomanry became a divisional regiment of the Royal Armoured Corps and trained with Cromwell and Comet tanks. Taking the salute is Maj.Gen. C.M. White, commanding Catterick District.

Between 1956 and 1967, the Shropshire Yeomanry served as a reconnaissance regiment, equipped firstly with Daimler armoured cars and scout cars and later with Ferrets. Here, they are shown with men of the 3rd Dragoon Guards (Carabineers) on exercise in 1962.

Men of the Shropshire Yeomanry in a Ferret scout car, run into an ambush laid by the 3rd Carabineers during exercises in 1962.

Winners of the 'best minor unit' cup in the Divisional Patrol Competition, Larkhill camp 1966, which included men of Shropshire RHA. Left to right, back row: Cpl. K. Willocks, Gnr Groom, Gnr Hutchinson, L/Bdr Turner. Front row: Bombardier Stiff, Capt. Ratcliffe, Sgt Adams, Bdr Soame.

Light Infantry Volunteers in training with helicopters at Okehampton, 1968. When the 4th KSLI was disbanded, The Light Infantry Volunteers (formed in 1967) took over their role as the county's Territorial infantry unit. In 1972 they became part of the 5th Light Infantry (Volunteers).

Light Infantry Volunteers training in Cyprus in 1967. Overseas training exercises were not such a novelty for the Territorial Army after the Second World War.

Light Infantry Volunteers practise landing from a DUKW ('Duck') at Okehampton in 1968. The soldier at front left carries the General Purpose Machine Gun, introduced in 1962; the others wear Combat Dress and carry the Self Loading Rifle.

Six

Special
Occasions

Officers of the 2nd Volunteer Battalion in camp in 1901. As was the custom of the time, they wear black crepe armbands as a symbol of mourning for the death of the sovereign: Queen Victoria had died on 22 January.

The Guard of Honour of 'C' Company, 4th (Territorial) Battalion, KSLI, mounted at Wellington Station in July 1909. In their new red serge dress uniforms, they await the arrival of Princess Marie Louise of Schleswig-Holstein. To the left centre are Maj. C.W. Leake, commanding 'C' Company, in the old uniform of the 2nd Volunteer Battalion and, in busby, Maj. R.D. Newill, commanding the Shropshire Royal Horse Artillery, in full dress (see also p. 49).

The Square and High Street, Shrewsbury: the Shropshire Yeomanry in full dress as mounted escort to HM King George V during his visit to Shrewsbury on 3 July 1914, when he attended the Horticultural Show. The mayor and civic dignitaries greet the King as he steps from his carriage. Lining the street to the right are the 4th KSLI, also in full dress.

Bangor University, July 1911: King George V (with Queen Mary to the left) presents new Colours to the 4th KSLI. Visible on the right is the Colour Party of the Shropshire Yeomanry, who had just been presented with their new Guidon. (The Guidon is now in the Regimental Museum in Shrewsbury Castle.)

Escort to the King: officers and senior NCO's of the Shropshire Yeomanry during the royal visit in 1914. Lt Croft and Lt Swire are seen slightly forward, to left and right.

Edward, Prince of Wales, takes the salute as the 4th KSLI march past. In the snow and biting cold near Cambrai just after the city had been recaptured by the Allies, in October 1918. The French Premier, M. Clemenceau was also present.

The presentation of the Fench Croix-de-Guerre avec Palme to 4th KSLI at the Quarry, Shrewsbury, June 1922. It was given in honour of their gallantry at Bligny in 1918. General Berthelot presented the medal, thereafter borne on the Regimental Colour, and also gave out cockades of Croix-de-Guerre ribbon to be worn on the left side of the cap.

Shropshire Yeomanry in full dress as part of the Mounted Procession during the Coronation of George VI in 1937. Left to right: Col. Sir Richard Leighton, Squadron Sgt-Maj. G. Gatensbury, Cpl W. Salter, Tpr H.E. Taylor. Dismounted men of the Shropshire Yeomanry formed part of the street-lining party.

Officers and men of 'B' Battery, 76th (Shropshire Yeomanry) Medium Regiment, Royal Artillery approaching St Mary's church, Welshpool, on Armistice Sunday in 1940.

The 5th (Wellington) Battalion, Shropshire Home Guard, being inspected by Maj.-Gen. D.P. Dickinson in 1944. This was the year in which the Home Guard was 'stood down'. The Shropshire Home Guard raised 11 battalions, with 31,000 men passing through its ranks.

The presentation in June 1947 of Illuminated Addresses by the Borough and County Councils to the Shropshire Regiments, in recognition of their distinguished war service. Left to right are detachments of the KSLI, the Shropshire Yeomanry and the Shropshire RHA.

Representatives of the Shropshire Yeomanry receiving from the Illuminated Address and a silver bugle in recognition of the Regiment's war services. These were presented by Lt-Gen. Sir Oliver Leese who had accepted the awards on their behalf in the ceremony above.

The Shropshire Yeomanry on parade outside Kirkcudbright Castle, Galloway, 1954. The Shropshire Yeomanry attended two consecutive camps in southern Scotland, training with tanks on the extensive Royal Armoured Corps ranges near Kirkcudbright. At this parade, the British Empire Medal was presented to SQMS W.E. Knott (who may be seen on the far right of the photograph on p. 6), who had served since 1926.

The Shropshire Royal Horse Artillery firing a 21-gun salute in the Quarry, Shrewsbury, to celebrate the Coronation of Queen Elizabeth II in 1953. The four 25-pounder guns were borrowed for the occasion from Park Hall camp, Oswestry.

The 50th anniversary of the formation of the Territorial Army (out of the old Volunteer units) was celebrated in 1958. The Mayor and army dignitaries take the salute during a march-past by elements of all of Shropshire's Territorial units on St Chad's Terrace. The town's Boer War memorial can be seen on the far left.

The detachment of 4th KSLI with Colours in St James's Park during the Golden Jubilee celebrations for the Territorial Army in 1958. Representatives of all the British Territorial units were present at a colourful review by the Queen in Hyde Park. From left to right, back row: L/Cpl P. Jones, Cpl T. Medlicott, Sgt Smith, Capt. Hone, Capt. Bratton, Lt Cock, Sgt Watkins, Sgt T. Allen, Cpl 'Blossom' Williams. Seated: WO R. Gough, WO P. Downward, WO W. Jones, Major Daborn, WO R. Williams, Col.-Sgt 'Punch' Rogers, Sgt J. Grindley. On the ground: Cpl E. Maun, Cpl T. Oswell, L/Cpl Pugh.

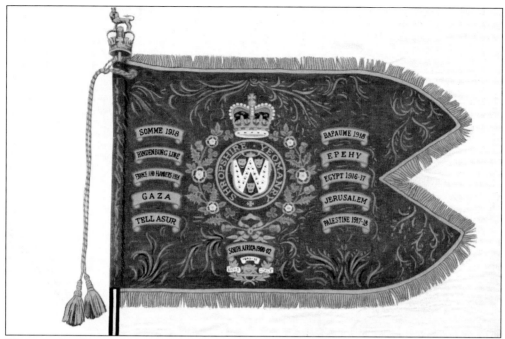

The new Guidon of the Shropshire Yeomanry, presented in June 1959. In addition to battle honours for South Africa 1900-1902 and 1914-18, it bears the Royal Artillery field-gun badge in commemoration of the Yeomanry's service as artillery during the Second World War.

Soldiers of the Shropshire Yeomanry on parade in the Quarry, Shrewsbury, during the ceremonies for the presentation of the new Guidon on 21 June 1959. The inspection was carried out by General Sir Francis Festing, Chief of the Imperial General Staff, who presented the new Colour.

The presentation of new Colours to the 4th KSLI by Princess Mary, in June 1964. Lt-Col A.F. Daborn stands with drawn sword to the left. In the event, these were the last colours of the 4th, which was disbanded only three years later.

Mrs D. Thellusson presents to Maj. P. Graham TD (right), commanding Shropshire RHA and Capt. B. Ratcliffe, the presentation sword and dress belt worn by her grandfather, Lt-Col. Field. The sword was given to Field in 1864 (see p. 45) and is now displayed in the Regimental Museum.

The last appearance of the Shropshire Royal Horse Artillery, as part of the street-lining party during the Queen's visit to open the new Shirehall in Shrewsbury on 22 March 1967. They were absorbed into the Shropshire Yeomanry shortly afterwards.

Laying up the Colours of the Shropshire Yeomanry. The Shropshire Yeomanry was briefly stood down in 1967, replaced by a Signal Company and a cadre. The cadre was expanded in 1971 as the Shropshire Yeomanry Squadron of the new Mercian Yeomanry and now forms part of the Royal Mercian and Lancastrian Yeomanry.

The Queen, escorted by Maj. S.E. Wardle, inspects the 4th KSLI at the opening of the new Shirehall in Shrewsbury in March 1967. This was the last ceremonial appearance of the old 4th (Territorial) Battalion, parading their Queen's Colour. They were disbanded a few weeks later. Their immediate successor as Territorial Army infantry in the county was The Light Infantry Volunteers.

The last of the Great War Yeomen: Mr George Pryke receives a painting from Capt D. Smith of the Shropshire Yeomanry Squadron, Royal Mercian and Lancastrian Yeomanry, on his 100th birthday in December 1993. Sgt M. Churm as Sword Orderly stands behind, in Shropshire Yeomanry full dress. A gamekeeper near Ellesmere for nearly seventy years, Mr Pryke was the last surviving Shropshire Yeoman of 1914-18 and the last surviving KSLI winner of the Military Medal, which he won with the 10th (Yeomanry) Battalion in France in 1918. He died on 21 January 1994.

Bugle Major Friend and L/Cpl Lowes sound the advance for Cpl Riley, Pte Dilnot, L/Cpl Rhodes, Lt Tomley. The 5 LI team took part in a 4,000 mile race from Southern Spain to the Arctic circle, to raise funds towards the re-construction of the Regimental Museum in Shrewsbury Castle in 1994.

Shropshire Yeomanry Squadron of the Royal Mercian and Lancastrian Yeomanry under Squadron Sgt-Maj. R. Sadler marching down High Street, during the celebration of the granting of the Freedom Shrewsbury in 1995. This year saw the 200th anniversary of the raising of the Shropshire Yeomanry.

The Queen and the Duke of Edinburgh inspect representatives of all the British Yeomanry regiments in Windsor Great Park in April 1994. This colourful Review was held to celebrate 200 years of the Yeomanry and included detachments of the Shropshire Yeomanry and 95 (Shropshire Yeomanry) Signal Squadron.

The re-opening of Shrewsbury Castle and Regimental Museum in May 1995. Shown here are (far left) Princess Alexandra, with the Shropshire Yeomanry Guidon under Warrant Officer Booth and Sgt M. Hughes, the colours of The Light Infantry, men of 95 (Shropshire Yeomanry) Signal Squadron and the Band and Bugles of 5 LI.

Full circle? Maj. Lindsay Wallace TD, Shropshire Yeomanry, Deputy Lieutenant of Shropshire and Chairman of the Trustees of the Shropshire Regimental Museum, introduces Princess Alexandra to men of the Loyal Newport Volunteers during the ceremonies at Shrewsbury Castle in 1995. This Civic Guard, founded in 1987 (see also p. 58), keeps alive the look and the traditions of at least one of the old Shropshire Volunteer units, in this case one originally formed in 1803 during the Napoleonic War.